Sam can jump over the stream.

Sam wants them all to jump over
the stream.

"Come on Jojo," says Sam.

"Come on Ben," says Jojo.

"Come on Mouse," says Ben.

Mouse does not want to jump.

Sam jumps…

and jumps

and jumps!

9

Oh no! What will Mouse do?

Sam is in the stream.

Mouse helps Sam.

Oh no! Mouse has cut his arm.

Mouse has a bad cut.

What will they do now?